✓ 03338

 May 99!

Minibeasts

Sally Morgan

Wayland

Titles in this series
Castles
Dinosaurs
Fairs and Circuses
Houses and Homes
Minibeasts
My Body
The Seasons
Transport

This book was prepared for Wayland (Publishers) Ltd
by Globe Education, Nantwich, Cheshire

Design concept by Pinpoint
Book design by Stephen Wheele Design
Artwork by Phil Weare

First published in 1995 by
Wayland (Publishers) Ltd
61 Western Road, Hove
East Sussex BN3 1JD

Printed and bound in Italy by
L. E. G. O. S.p.A., Vincenza

British Library Cataloguing in Publication Data

Morgan, Sally
Minibeasts. – (Topic Box Series)
I. Title II. Series
592

ISBN 0 7502 1604 2

Picture acknowledgements

Bruce Coleman 10 (Jan Taylor), 11 and cover (Dr Frieder Sauer), 23 (Jane Burton)
Ecoscene 7b (Wilkinson), 12/13 (Sally Morgan), 14 (Robin Williams), 16 (Cooper), 17 (Greenwood), 20 (Robin Williams),
25 (Gryniewicz), 27 (Ian Beames)
NHPA 7t (Peter Parks), 8/9 (Stephen Dalton), 9 (Stephen Dalton), 12 (G I Bernard), 19t (Stephen Dalton),
19b (Stephen Dalton), 21 (G I Bernard)
Oxford Scientific Films 15 (Breck P Kent), 26 (Katnie Atkinson)
Wayland Picture Library 4, 24

Contents

What are Minibeasts? 4

How Small? 6

Insects 8

Beetles 10

Bees and Wasps 12

Flies and Maggots 14

Butterflies 16

Jumping Insects 18

Centipedes, Millipedes 20

Spiders 22

Snails and Slugs 24

Worms 26

Living in Leaf Litter 28

Word List 30

Finding Out More 31

Index 32

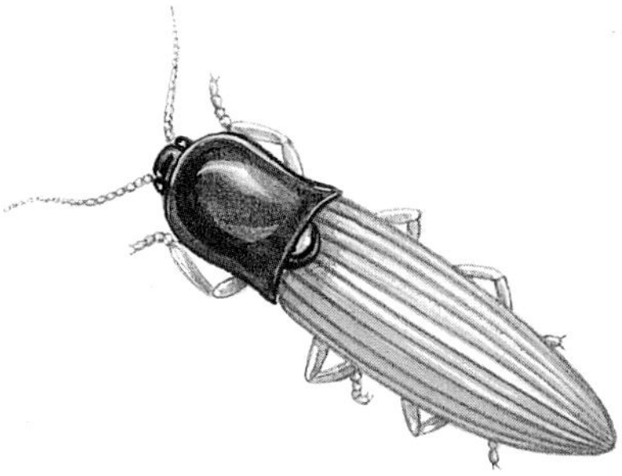

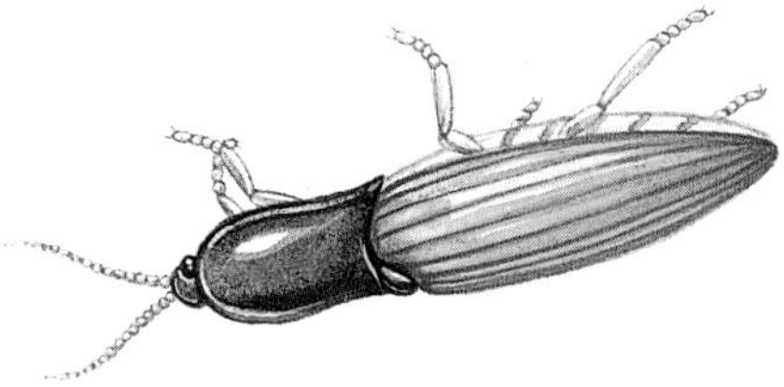

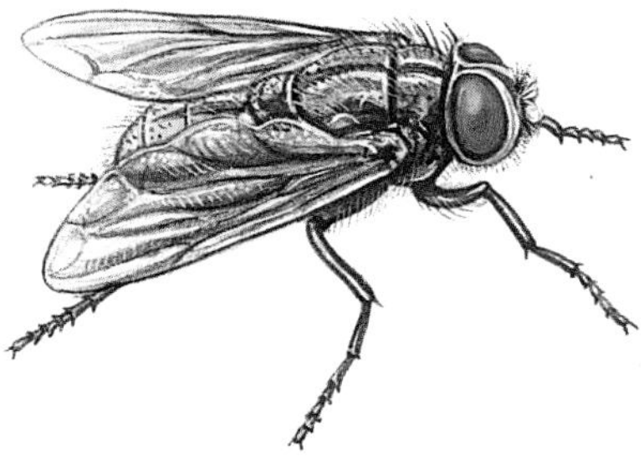

What are Minibeasts?

Minibeasts are small animals. Some people call them creepy crawlies. They are found everywhere – in the ground, in our homes and in water.

Minibeasts are invertebrate animals. That means that, unlike people, they do not have a backbone.

The biggest group of invertebrates is the insects. But there are also spiders, millipedes, snails, worms and many others.

common blue

small white

(Left) Some minibeasts, such as this water scorpion, are aquatic. They are specially adapted to living in water.

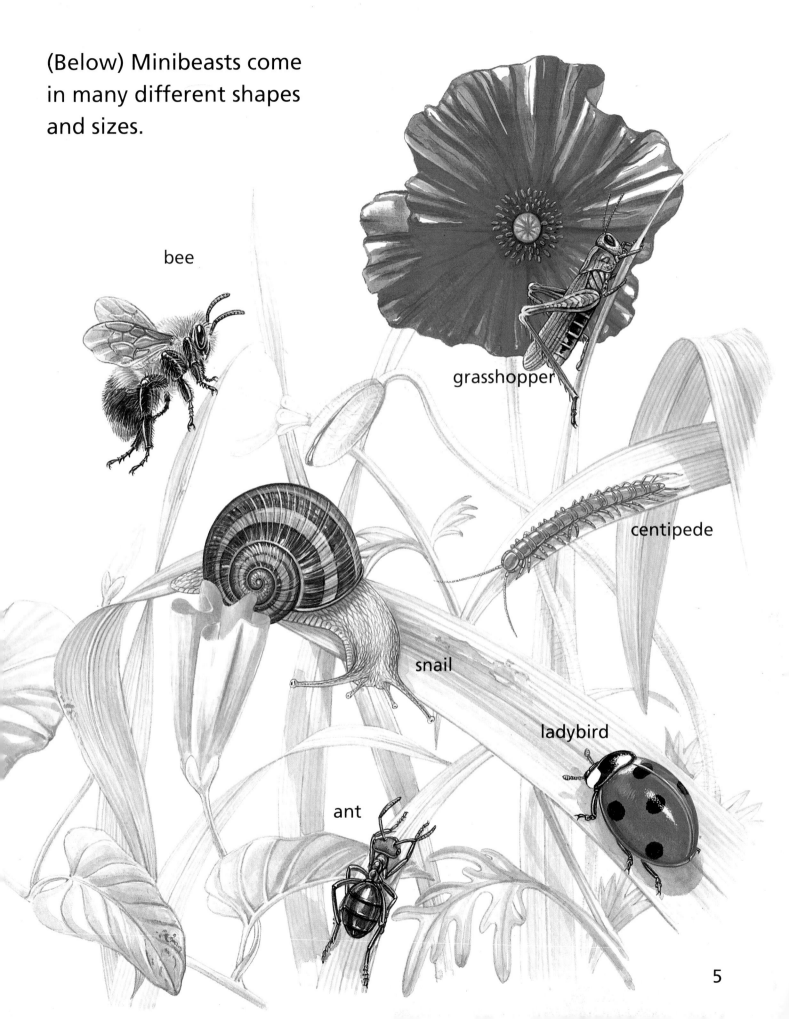

(Below) Minibeasts come in many different shapes and sizes.

bee

grasshopper

centipede

snail

ladybird

ant

5

How Small?

The smallest minibeasts are difficult
to see easily with our eyes. So we have
to use a magnifying glass.

A magnifying glass has a specially shaped
piece of glass or plastic called a lens. This
makes things look much larger. Lenses are
also found in telescopes and binoculars.

Some minibeasts can only be seen using
a microscope. A microscope contains
many lenses which make the minibeast
seem hundreds of times larger.

(Right) Ants are tiny
insects that are difficult
to see without a
magnifying glass.

(Left) You may share your bed with thousands of tiny minibeasts which which are far too small to be seen. Under a microscope bed bugs look quite frightening.

(Right) Many minibeasts live in water. These children are pond dipping. They catch the animals in nets and identify them before putting them back.

Insects

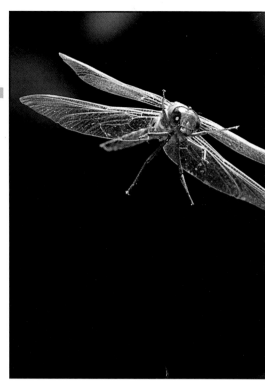

Insects are small. Even the largest insect is barely 15 centimetres long. All insects have six legs and many have wings so they can fly.

Insects do not have bones inside their bodies like people. Instead they have a tough outer covering which protects their body. This has to be shed to allow the insect to grow.

There are more kinds of insect than any other animal.

(Above) Insects usually have two pairs of wings which beat up and down when they fly.

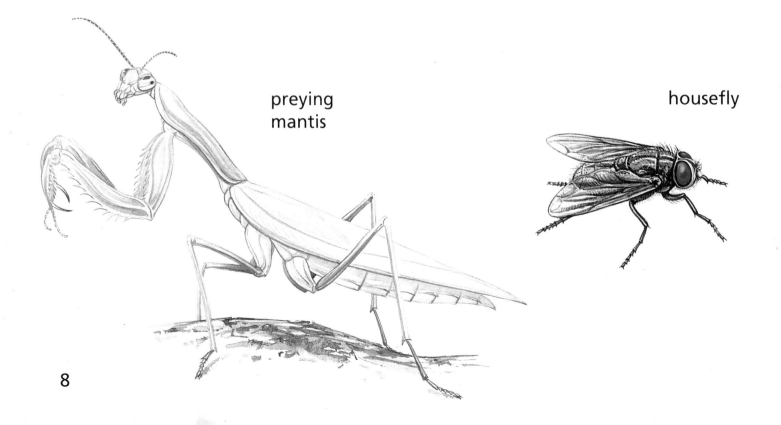

preying
mantis

housefly

(Below) Although insects look very different they all have six legs and three parts to their bodies.

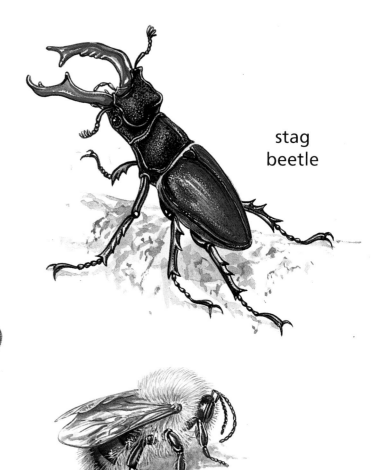

stag beetle

tiger moth

honey bee

(Left) Each eye of an insect is made up of thousands of tiny eyes. This type of eye is called a compound eye. Insects see a very different world to human beings.

Beetles

Beetles have two pairs of wings, but the front pair is stiff, forming a hard case. This protects the delicate pair of hindwings underneath which are used for flying.

Beetles have strong jaws which act like pincers. The beetle uses them to bite its prey.

Some beetles are very useful insects. Ladybirds eat greenflies which is helpful if they are in your garden.

(Left) Many beetles, such as this giant stag beetle from Borneo, have extremely tough coverings that protect them from predators.

(Right) When beetles visit flowers, they become covered with pollen which they carry to other flowers. This helps the flowers to make seeds.

(Above) Dung beetles roll dung into small balls. They bury the dung and then lay an egg in it. When the larva hatches it has plenty of food.

Bees and Wasps

Bees make honey and pollinate flowers. Honey bees live in large groups called colonies and feed on pollen and nectar.

Honey bees make the nectar into honey in their special 'honey stomach'. They also make wax, which they use to build their hive.

The bright black and yellow colours of bees and wasps are a warning that they can sting. A bee will die after stinging, but a wasp will live on.

(Above) Wasps are attracted to the sugar contained in fallen apples.

(Right) A bee visits a flower to collect pollen and nectar. The end of its tube-like mouth looks like a spoon. It is ideal for sucking up sugary nectar.

The male bees are called drones.

(Right) Inside the hive bees build cells made of wax.

Only the queen bee can lay eggs. Most of her eggs, which are cared for by the workers, develop into new workers. There is only one queen bee in a hive.

Workers are female bees that collect pollen and nectar from flowers and carry them to the hive. They also build their hive.

Flies And Maggots

Flies are found everywhere. Unlike most insects they only have one pair of wings.

Many flies feed on the blood of other animals. Midges, mosquitoes and horse-flies all bite people. The female fly needs a meal of blood before she can lay her eggs.

Bluebottles and houseflies lay their eggs on meat and dead bodies. The larvae are called maggots.

(Right) If you glance quickly, this hoverfly looks like a wasp. Hoverflies have mimicked the warning colours of wasps, but they do not have a sting.

(Right) Flies lay their eggs on meat. After a few days the maggots hatch out. They feed on the meat and soon pupate, turning into adult flies.

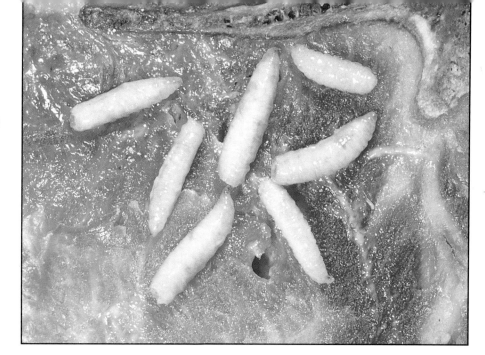

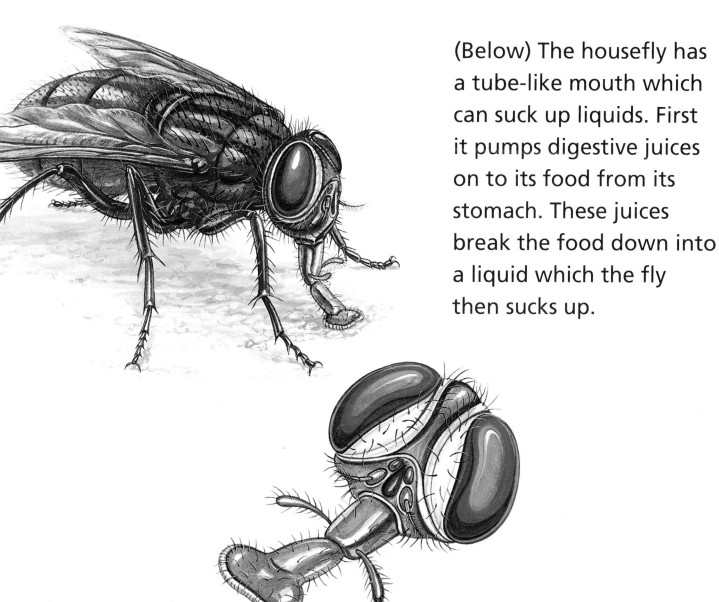

(Below) The housefly has a tube-like mouth which can suck up liquids. First it pumps digestive juices on to its food from its stomach. These juices break the food down into a liquid which the fly then sucks up.

Butterflies

A butterfly has large, colourful wings covered in tiny scales and a very long, thin tube-like tongue that is coiled up when not in use. The butterfly extends its tongue into flowers to suck up the nectar.

Butterfly eggs hatch to caterpillars. A caterpillar spends its life eating and growing. When it has grown enough, it turns into a pupa and begins to change into an adult butterfly. This change is called metamorphosis.

The small tortoiseshell butterfly lays her eggs on nettles which the caterpillars eat once they hatch.

(Left and right) Brightly coloured butterflies live in rainforests in the tropical areas of the world near the Equator.

The life cycle of the small tortoiseshell butterfly.

The caterpillars grow fast, so they have to shed their skin several times.

After the last moult, the caterpillar covers itself with silk and turns into a chrysalis. Inside the chrysalis, the caterpillar changes into an adult butterfly which breaks out of the chrysalis case and flies away.

17

Jumping Insects

Jumping insects have long legs. Grasshoppers and locusts have very long and powerful back legs with which to propel themselves into the air.

Springtails are tiny insects with special forked springs at the end of their abdomens. When the springs are released, they push the insects forward.

Of all the jumping insects, fleas, springtails and grasshoppers are the record holders.

(Right) If you disturb a click beetle, it falls on its back and pretends to be dead! Then suddenly, it catapults into the air, twists so that it lands the right way up and runs away.

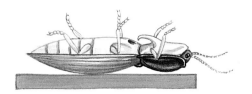

(Right) A grasshopper begins to jump. Its long hind legs are extended giving a good lift-off.

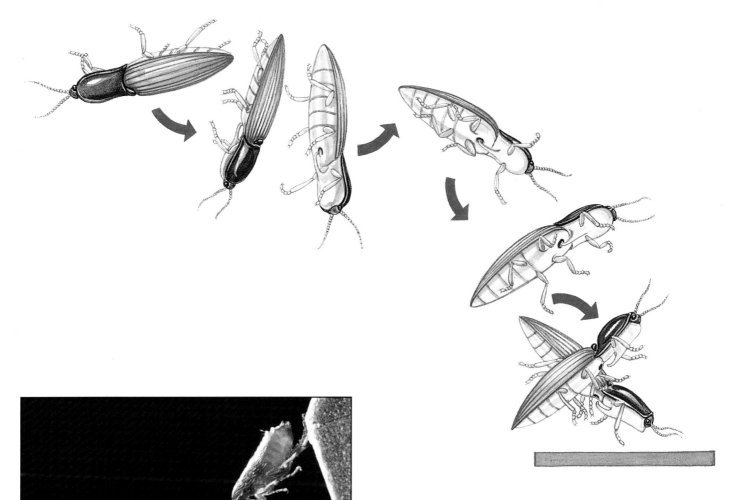

(Left) Fleas can jump 150 times their own body length. If humans could do this, they would be able to jump half a kilometre.

Centipedes, Millipedes

Centipedes are night time animals. They do not have any eyes, but do have an excellent sense of touch and smell. The word 'centipede' means 100 legs but some may have as many a 254 legs.

'Millipede' means a thousand legs but even the largest millipedes only have 750 legs. They crawl along the ground with long wavy movements. They feed on leaves and decaying plants.

(Left) Centipedes are fearsome predators that hunt small invertebrates. They have a powerful pair of poison jaws that they use to both bite and paralyse their prey.

(Left) Some millipedes roll up into a protective ball when threatened, just like a hedgehog rolls up to protect itself from attack.

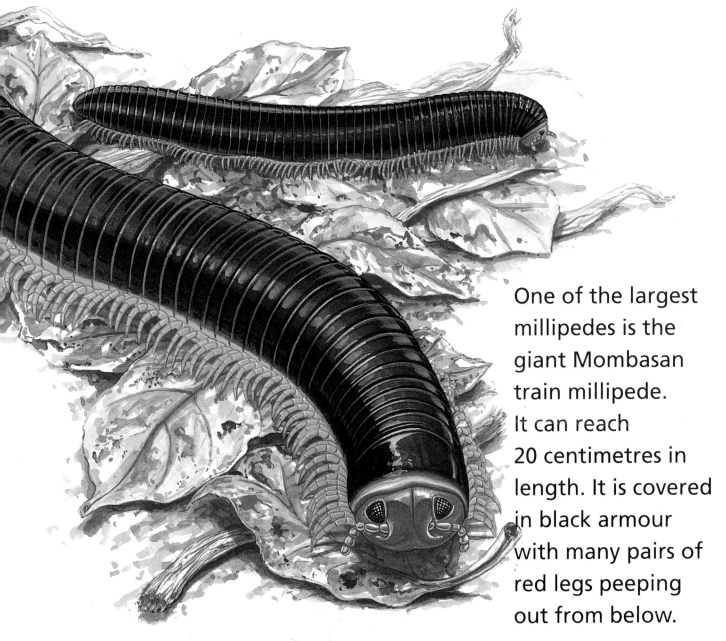

One of the largest millipedes is the giant Mombasan train millipede. It can reach 20 centimetres in length. It is covered in black armour with many pairs of red legs peeping out from below.

Spiders

Spiders may be small animals, but they scare people! They can move quickly on their eight legs. They are not insects, but belong to a group called arachnids, which also includes scorpions and ticks.

Spiders are hunters and prey on small invertebrates. They have a special jaw which injects poison into the bodies of their prey. Some spiders build traps out of spider silk to trap their prey.

(Right) Scorpions are relatives of spiders.

A scorpion has a long tail with a sting at the end and a powerful pair of jaws to catch its prey.

(Left) Spiders can spin silk which they use to make a web. Some of the silk is sticky, so that any insect flying into the web is trapped. The frantic movements of the trapped insect attract the spider.

(Below) Some of the larger spiders, like this tarantula are covered with hairs.

crab spider

wolf spider

(Above) Spiders have eight legs, but only two body parts, a head and an abdomen. They do not have large compound eyes, like insects but eight simple eyes.

tarantula

Snails and Slugs

Snails and slugs are very slow-moving animals. They are herbivores which means they eat plant leaves and they can do a lot of damage to farmers' crops and garden plants.

Snails have shells which protect their soft bodies. Their home is their shell and they carry it around all the time.

Slugs do not have a shell outside their bodies, although there is the remains of a shell deep inside.

(Below right) The world's largest land snail is the giant African land snail. It is huge compared with the common garden snail.

(Left) Snails and slugs are found in damp, dark places. They are most active at night especially if it is wet.

(Left) These spotted kerry slugs (up to 10 centimetres long) are feeding on dead leaves in a wood. As they glide forwards, they leave a glistening, slimy trail behind them.

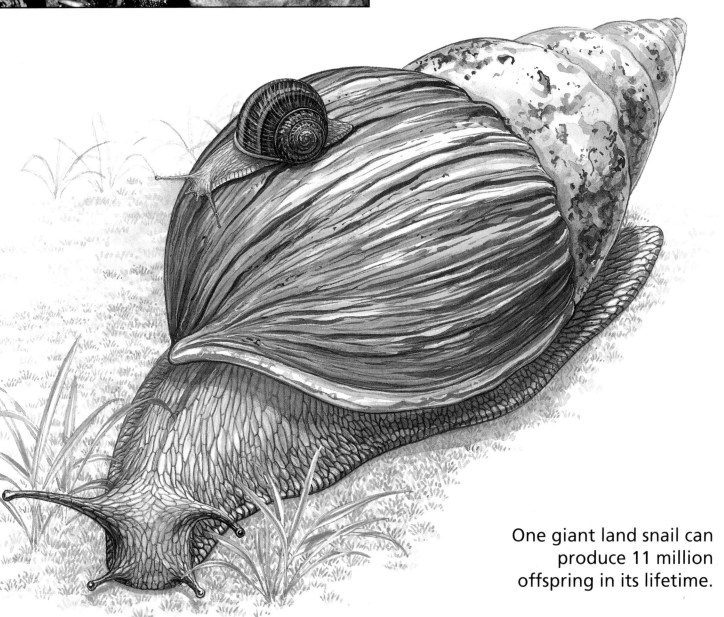

One giant land snail can produce 11 million offspring in its lifetime.

Worms

Earthworms are long, thin animals with bodies made up of many identical segments, joined end on end. Giant worms in Australia reach over two metres in length.

Worms do not have any bones. Instead their body is filled with a fluid. They move by stretching and contracting. They eat dead and decaying matter they find in the soil. Earthworms help to mix the soil and their burrows aerate and drain it.

(Below) Once soil has passed through an earthworm's body, the worm leaves the soil as a worm cast near the entrance to its burrow.

(Below) Many marine worms, such as this fireworm, are brightly coloured.

(Left) Robins like to feed their young broods on worms, but they have to be quick to catch a worm before it disappears into its burrow.

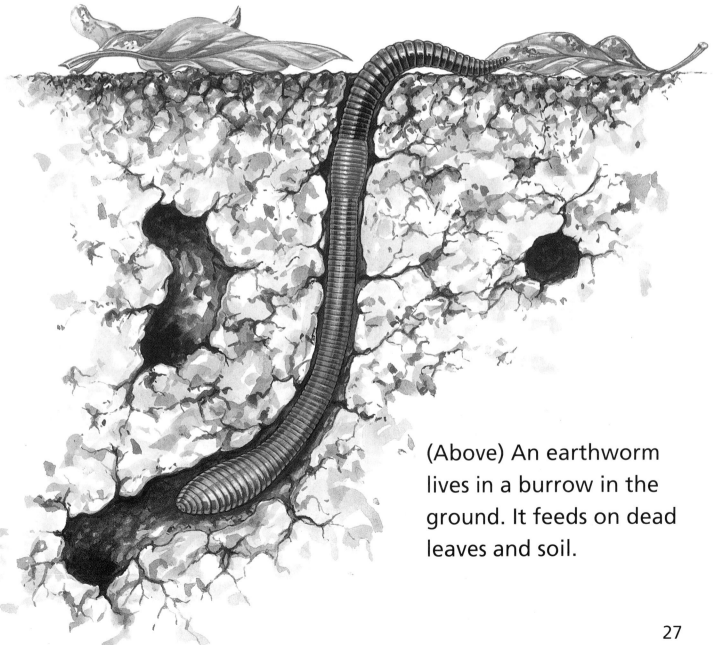

(Above) An earthworm lives in a burrow in the ground. It feeds on dead leaves and soil.

Living in Leaf Litter

In woodlands, the surface of the soil is covered with a thick layer of dead leaves and fallen twigs. It might not look very interesting, but it is alive with hundreds of different kinds of minibeasts.

Many are too small to see but you can usually spot herbivores such as slugs and snails feeding on the decaying leaves. They are hunted by spiders and centipedes that move among the leaves looking for prey.

A tree stump surrounded by dead leaves is home to many different animals and plants. These animals form a community that is specially suited to living in the leaf litter.

wood-louse

ants

snail

mole

Moles prey on worms and beetles

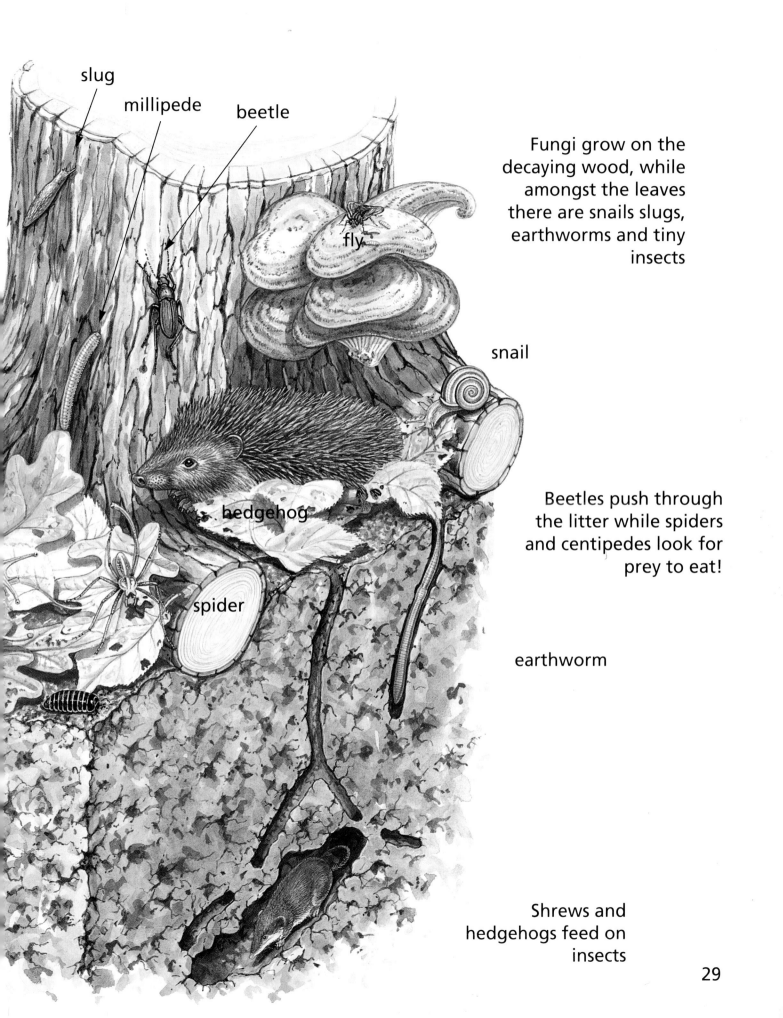

slug

millipede

beetle

fly

Fungi grow on the decaying wood, while amongst the leaves there are snails slugs, earthworms and tiny insects

snail

hedgehog

Beetles push through the litter while spiders and centipedes look for prey to eat!

spider

earthworm

Shrews and hedgehogs feed on insects

29

Word List

Abdomen The section of an insect or spider which is furthest from the head.

Aerate To allow air to pass through.

Aquatic Living in water.

Arachnophobia A fear of spiders.

Backbone A bony rod running down the back of an animal which gives support.

Carnivorous Meat-eating.

Caterpillar The larval stage in the life cycle of a butterfly, which feeds on plants.

Chrysalis The stage in the life cycle of a butterfly during which the caterpillar turns into an adult.

Colony A large group of animals living together.

Community A group of plants and animals living together in a habitat.

Decaying Breaking down, rotting.

Digestive To do with making food break up more easily.

Dung Animal waste.

Herbivore An animal which eats only plants.

Hive The place where bees live.

Invertebrate An animal which does not have a backbone.

Larva The young stage of an invertebrate that looks very different to the adult.

Lens A piece of glass or plastic with a curved surface which focuses light to make things look much larger (or smaller).

Maggot The name given to the larvae of some flies.

Magnifying Making larger.

Metamorphosis The changes in form that some animals go through as they grow.

Microscope An instrument through which you can see very small objects.

Mimicked Copied, the imitation of one animal by another.

Moult To shed a skin.

Nectar Sugary liquid produced by plants.

Nocturnal Animals which are active by night.

Paralyse To make helpless.

Pincers Sharp jaws which grip firmly.

Poison A substance which will kill a living organism.

Finding Out More

Places to Visit

Butterfly House, Syon Park, Isleworth, London

Creepy Crawlies exhibit Natural History Museum Cromwell Road London SW7 5BD

New Forest Butterfly Farm, Longdown, Ashurst near Southampton Hampshire

The insect house at your nearest zoo or wildlife park.

Books to Read

Bugs Beetles and Other Insects, John Feltwell, (OUP, 1992)

Eyewitness Explorers: Insects, (Dorling Kindersley, 1992)

Eyewitness Explorers: Butterflies and Moths, (Dorling Kindersley, 1993)

Fun with Science: Minibeasts, Rosie Harlow and Gareth Morgan (Kingfisher, 1991)

Keeping Minibeasts series – Twelve titles (Watts)

Lift Off: Insects, Joy Richardson (Watts, 1991)

Nature Projects: Keeping Minibeasts, Stephen Savage, (Wayland, 1995)

Observing Nature: Butterfly, Stephen Savage, (Wayland, 1994)

Observing Nature, Spider, Stephen Savage, (Wayland, 1995)

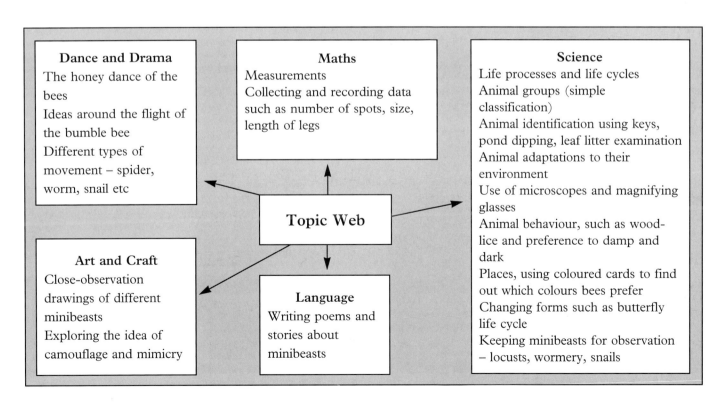

Dance and Drama
The honey dance of the bees
Ideas around the flight of the bumble bee
Different types of movement – spider, worm, snail etc

Art and Craft
Close-observation drawings of different minibeasts
Exploring the idea of camouflage and mimicry

Maths
Measurements
Collecting and recording data such as number of spots, size, length of legs

Topic Web

Language
Writing poems and stories about minibeasts

Science
Life processes and life cycles
Animal groups (simple classification)
Animal identification using keys, pond dipping, leaf litter examination
Animal adaptations to their environment
Use of microscopes and magnifying glasses
Animal behaviour, such as wood-lice and preference to damp and dark
Places, using coloured cards to find out which colours bees prefer
Changing forms such as butterfly life cycle
Keeping minibeasts for observation – locusts, wormery, snails

Index

Page numbers in **bold** *show that there is an illustration on that page.*

ants **5**, 6, **6-7**, 28
arachnids 22

bed bug 7
bees 5, 12, **12**
   drone **13**
   hive 12, **13**, 30
   honey stomach 12
   queen **13**
   wax 12, **13**
   worker **13**
beetles 10, **11**, 29
   jaws 10
   pincers 10, 30
   wings 10
butterflies 16
   caterpillar 16, **16-17**, 30
   chrysalis 17, 30
   eggs 16, **16**
   life cycle **16-17**
   scales 16

centipedes 5, 20, **20**, 28
click beetle **18-19**
common blue 4
crab spider 23
creepie crawlies 4

dung beetles **10-11**

earthworms 26, **26**, 27

fleas 18, **19**

flies 14, **29**
   greenflies 10
   horse flies 14
   housefly **8**, **15**
   hoverfly **14**
   maggots 14, **15**, 30
   midges 14
   mosquitoes 14
   mouth **15**
   wings 14

giant African land snail 25
giant Mombasan train
   millipede **20-21**
giant worms 26
grasshoppers 5, 18, **19**

herbivores 24, 28, 30
honey bee **9**, 12, **13**

insects 4, 8, 14, 22, **29**
   compound eye **9**
   jumping 18, **18-19**, **19**
   wings 8, **8-9**, 30
invertebrate 4, **20**, 22, 30

kerry slugs 25

ladybirds 5, 10
leaf litter 28, **28-9**
locusts 18

magnifying glass 6, **6**
marine fireworm 26
metamorphosis 16, 30
microscope 6, 30
millipedes 4, 20, **21**, 29

nectar 12 **12**, 16, 30

people 4, 8
pollen **11**, 12, **12**, 30
pond dipping 7
predators **10**, 20
prey **20**, 22, 28, **28**
preying mantis 8

scorpion 22, **22**
slugs 24, 28, **29**
small tortoiseshell **16-17**
small white **4**
snails 4, 5, 24, **24**, 28, **28**, 29
   shells 24
spiders 4, 22, **23**, 28, **29**
   eyes 23
   legs 22
   silk 22, **23**
   web 23
springtails 18
stag beetle **9**, 10

tarantula 23
ticks 22
tiger moth **9**
tropical butterflies **16**, 17

wasps 12, **12-13**, 14
water scorpion 4
wolf spider 23
woodlands 28
wood-louse 28
worms 4, 26, **26**, 27, **28-9**
   segments 26, 30
   worm cast 26